LACROSSE

Facing Off on the Field

PREPARING FOR GAME DAY

BASEBALL & SOFTBALL: SUCCESS ON THE DIAMOND

BASKETBALL: STRATEGY ON THE HARDWOOD

CHEERLEADING: TECHNIQUES FOR PERFORMING

EXTREME SPORTS: POINTERS FOR PUSHING THE LIMITS

FOOTBALL: TOUGHNESS ON THE GRIDIRON

LACROSSE: FACING OFF ON THE FIELD

SOCCER: BREAKING AWAY ON THE PITCH

TRACK & FIELD: CONDITIONING FOR GREATNESS

VOLLEYBALL: APPROACHING THE NET

WRESTLING: CONTENDING ON THE MAT

PREPARING FOR GAME DAY

LACROSSE
Facing Off on the Field

Peter Douglas

MASON CREST

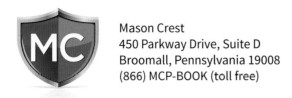

Mason Crest
450 Parkway Drive, Suite D
Broomall, Pennsylvania 19008
(866) MCP-BOOK (toll free)

First printing
9 8 7 6 5 4 3 2 1

ISBN (hardback) 978-1-4222-3918-6
ISBN (series) 978-1-4222-3912-4
ISBN (ebook) 978-1-4222-7873-4

Cataloging-in-Publication Data on file with the Library of Congress

QR CODES AND LINKS TO THIRD-PARTY CONTENT

CONTENTS

KEY ICONS TO LOOK FOR:

Words to understand: These words with their easy-to-understand definitions will increase the reader's understanding of the text while building vocabulary skills.

Sidebars: This boxed material within the main text allows readers to build knowledge, gain insights, explore possibilities, and broaden their perspectives by weaving together additional information to provide realistic and holistic perspectives.

Educational Videos: Readers can view videos by scanning our QR codes, providing them with additional educational content to supplement the text. Examples include news coverage, moments in history, speeches, iconic sports moments and much more!

Text-dependent questions: These questions send the reader back to the text for more careful attention to the evidence presented there.

Research projects: Readers are pointed toward areas of further inquiry connected to each chapter. Suggestions are provided for projects that encourage deeper research and analysis.

Series glossary of key terms: This back-of-the book glossary contains terminology used throughout this series. Words found here increase the reader's ability to read and comprehend higher-level books and articles in this field.

WORDS TO UNDERSTAND:

measured: done with thought and care

trans fats: a type of fat that is found especially in some vegetable oils and that is bad for health

velocity: quickness of motion

Chapter 1

GAME DAY

Lacrosse is not for everyone. It is high intensity and full contact, and a player will need full appreciation of both those aspects to excel. For those who have that appreciation, however, there is nothing like game day. When it is time to take the field, players want to be sure they are ready to perform at their best.

EQUIPMENT PREP

The night before the game, take some time to get everything you need to take with you prepped and ready to go. Check all of your gear and equipment, including stick strings, shoes and laces, mouth guard, and all pads. Keep a checklist handy to help you remember everything you need to take, including snacks.

"I can't control my size and speed at a young age, but you can control your stick skills, your shooting, your accuracy, stuff like that. Working on that stuff at a young age and being very critical of myself when it came to that stuff, when that size and speed came, it allowed me to put my whole game together."

– Rob Pannell, two-time Enners Award winner and Tewaarton Award winner

SLEEP WELL

Getting all packed up and prepared to head to the field will give players fewer things to

Ice cream and other foods made with refined sugar are full of calories and lacking in nutrients. Athletes should avoid them.

think about, which will hopefully allow them to get a good night's sleep before the game. Experts recommend at least seven hours of sleep, but athletes should be in the habit of getting the proper sleep every night, not just the nights preceding games.

EAT TO COMPETE

Lacrosse is similar to soccer in that it includes both periods of high-intensity sprinting, with some explosive movements incorporated, in between extended periods of sustained running or jogging. Other than at the goaltending position, there should not be a lot of standing around in a well-played game.

Given this, players need fuel for both quick energy bursts and for endurance. To that end, players should eat a hearty meal the night before a morning or afternoon game

> 66 The easiest way to pick up a loose ball is to have your stick parallel to the floor. That way you can just run directly through it. If you can drop your back hand when you go in for these loose balls and get parallel as much as possible to the floor it will allow you to just scoop right through the ball. 99
>
> – Paul Rabil,
>   two-time MLL MVP

or on the morning of an evening game. That meal should be mostly comprised of carbohydrates, the substance the body uses to create energy. The exact amount of each nutrient depends on the weight of the athlete, but carbs should make up about 65 percent of that pregame lacrosse meal. These carbs should be of the complex variety. Good sources of complex carbs include fruits and vegetables, whole grain bread and pasta, oatmeal, bread, beans, and potatoes. Poor carb choices are foods that are made with refined flour and sugar, such as white bread and pasta, cereal, baked goods, crackers, ice cream, or candy. These simple carbohydrates are full of calories and provide little nutritional value.

Another 20 percent of the meal should come from healthy fats. Like carbs, there are good and bad kinds of fat. The fats athletes want come from nuts like almonds, peanut butter, eggs, and avocados. Foods with what are known as saturated or **trans fats** should be avoided.

> *"Take a disciplined approach to off-field weight training, nutrition and flexibility to avoid unnecessary injuries and to keep up with the growing pace and athleticism of our sport."*
>
> *– Jeff Tambroni, Penn State men's head coach*

The final 15 percent of the meal should consist of protein, which is also found in the eggs, nuts, and beans already mentioned. Further sources include lean meat like turkey or chicken breast, fish, and Greek yogurt.

About four hours before game time, players should eat a small meal, such as an egg with wheat toast, oatmeal with fruit, or whole wheat pasta. About an hour before the game, a small, high-carb snack, such as a banana, should top off the fuel reserves to get through the game.

H2O

Drinking lots of water during the game is necessary and important, but a good hydration plan starts well before it is time to lace up your cleats. A serious athlete should have good hydration habits at all times, but on game days specifically, drinking about twenty ounces of water within two hours of the opening face-off is recommended. During the game, players should try

Teams should keep plenty of water on hand to help players stay hydrated on hot days.

to drink another sixteen to twenty-four ounces, more if the weather is hot.

WARM-UP

Even on hot days, it is important to warm up the body and especially its muscles. The most important part of the warm-up is stretching. After the pregame snack and drink, players should start the warm-up with twenty-five minutes of stretching. Stretching loosens the muscles and tendons, increasing flexibility and therefore reducing the chance of injury. Stretching, along with staying hydrated, also helps prevent cramping. Lacrosse uses all of the body's muscle groups, so the routine should include both upper and lower body stretching, but it is especially important not to rush through the lower body stretching, such as in the groin, calves, and hamstrings. Stretching out the back muscles, both upper and lower, is also important.

DRILLS

After stretching, it is a good idea to get some stick work in. Make sure that the drills are dynamic and keep the body moving, so it does not cool back down and tighten up. Pass and catch drills that include running to scoop ground balls are good examples of dynamic drills.

Another example of a pregame drill is the tiger drill. For this offensive drill, two attackers

66 Every time the ball is transitioned from offensive player to offensive player (defenders) need to be talking. What's your assignment? Where's the ball? Are you the hot guy? Are you the second slot? If you talk on defense it's going to be tough for your coach to sit you on the bench. 99

– Quint Kessenich,
two-time Kelly Award winner

"What makes a dodger very effective is that they never plan their dodge. They make one hard move, they read what their defender does, and then they react off of what their defender does."

– Katie Chrest, 2005
Tewaarton Award winner

Scooping ground balls should be part of dynamic drills that take place during warm-ups.

and two midfielders square off against three defenders in a four-on-three situation. The four offensive players form a box shape around the goal. Those four players will be defended by the three defenders, with the offensive players looking to continually and quickly move the ball to the open player to set up an easy shot from in front of the goal.

In the cutters and feeders offensive drill, midfielders form two lines at the top end hash marks of the box, while attackers form two lines at the hash marks down low. The first midfielder starts by cutting at the attacker opposite the goal from him or her in a ready position to receive a pass. The attacker throws a pass that the midfielder can catch in stride on the same line. The midfielder catches and shoots, and the next midfielder in line then starts the sequence over.

A good drill to include for defensive players is long passing. Long passes will not have been covered in the initial pass and catch drill. Defenders should team up in pairs, and each partner should stand about thirty yards (twenty-seven meters) from the other. Each pair should then

"I want to make sure I get the stick low, below the top of my head, if possible below my chin. I want to keep it in tight. I want to bring my elbow up to protect the backside. I want to position my hand so I get a good tight cradle, and then I'm going to keep my body in between (the stick and defender)."

– Gary Gait,
Syracuse University
women's head coach
and six-time NLL MVP

spend five minutes throwing the ball back and forth, focusing on accuracy and **velocity**.

Another defensive drill is to work on stick checking. Defenders form a line standing side by side about five yards (between four and five meters) from each other. Each player holds the stick vertically out in front of his or her body, grasping it with one hand where the pocket meets the shaft. The first player in the line steps out and faces the player beside him or her. He or she then shuffles down the line, stick checking the dangling shafts of each player in the line, and then assumes the original position after reaching the end of the line. The next defender then steps out and repeats the process.

"When we're shooting from the inside, its important that we don't have to take the time to wind up to get a really hard shot on cage. It's not about power here, it's about accuracy."

– Jen Adams,
all-time NCAA leader
in career points

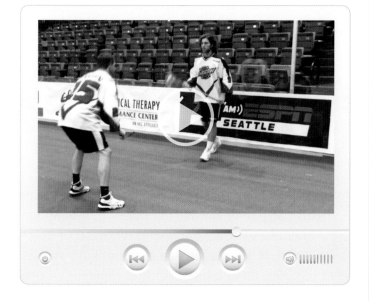

Check out this pro tip on how to play one-on-one defense.

Mistakes can lead to turnovers, and turnovers can lead to goals for the opponent. Mentally strong players cannot let mistakes affect them.

MENTAL APPROACH

Players also need to use the time before the game to get their minds into game mode. One way to do this is to use the time spent stretching the body to prepare the mind. During warm-ups, both teams will likely be out on the field. Pay attention to what the other team is doing, and notice what the players' roles are. Concentrate on the players whose roles will likely cause them to cross paths with you during the game, and study their tendencies. If you are an offensive player, watch the goaltender, and try to pick up any weak spots or habits he or she has. If you are a defender, watch the offensive players, and notice how they carry the ball, face-off tendencies, or which way they prefer to cut—anything that might give you a mental edge in the game.

Mental toughness can give teams and players a decided advantage. Being mentally tough means having the ability to focus on the task to come and to prevent your mind from wandering while out on the field. Nothing will distract you from performing your role for your team. Mental toughness also means that you will not allow mistakes to carry over to the rest of the game. Making mistakes is part of playing lacrosse or any sport. If the player you are checking scores, or you make a turnover that results in a goal against your team, you cannot let that get in your head. Have confidence that you will

> 66 Cutting off someone's dominant hand does not mean putting your stick on the side that you don't want them to go. It means taking it away, daring them to beat you with their weak hand. 99
>
> – Brett Hughes, two-time All-American and 2003 NCAA national champion

make the correct play the next time, and forget about things that have already happened as they cannot be changed.

Many players use the technique of imagery to help prepare them mentally to play the game. Using this technique, players visualize themselves succeeding in their minds before doing it on the field. Whether it is scoring a goal, making a save, or scooping every ground ball, players should imagine what that will look, sound, and feel like. They then go over it again and again until it is vivid in their minds. The theory is that the more vivid the scenario is in your mind, the more quickly you will react to it when it arises in the game. You will react rather than think, giving you an advantage over your opponent.

If you are one of the team leaders, and your coach allows it, you can help get yourself

"When it comes to game time, I just need to make sure that I'm mentally prepared, because if I've done the physical preparation, I just need to make sure I'm mentally prepared, I'm confident, and I'm zoned in for the game."

– Kristen Kjellman, two-time Tewaarton Award winner

A pregame pep talk from the coach or team leader can inspire confidence in the team.

> *"Go to the goal hard. Pick a spot on net and put the ball there. You can't get too fancy inside because the defense will be there trying to tear your head off."*

— *Mike Powell, four-time Turnbull Award winner*

> "I wanted to be a tough, hard-nosed attackman because I don't think you see that very much. It's something more than scoring goals and getting assists. It's a tangible asset that a coach can see."

– *Matt Danowski, two-time Enners Award winner and Tewaarton Award winner*

and your team in the game with a pep talk. The coach may choose to do this his- or herself. Confidence is an important component of an athlete's makeup, and this talk should serve to instill the team with the belief that they are going to win. Some talks can be fiery, while others are more **measured**. The goal of either variety is to ensure the team that if they play as well as they have prepared, they will win the game. Coaches will likely run through offensive sets and key opponent weaknesses separately. This talk should be motivational in nature, using any element that may provide that extra push for the team. Remind those who do not play often that their teammates feed off the positive energy they bring to the bench. Encourage players to trust in the hard work they have put in and to stick to the game plan that is tailored to their strengths. If everyone sticks to what they do well and lets their teammates do their jobs, success is inevitable.

Before you step on the field, be focused, be confident, and be prepared.

TEXT-DEPENDENT QUESTIONS:

1. How is lacrosse similar to soccer?

2. Give an example of a pregame drill.

3. What type of toughness can give teams and players a decided advantage?

RESEARCH PROJECT:

Create a pregame routine for yourself. Think through each aspect, and outline specific numbers of repetitions for drills, shots taken, and so on. Outline meals, rest, and all the necessary components that you feel could help best prepare you before a big game.

WORDS TO UNDERSTAND:

camaraderie: a feeling of good friendship among the people in a group

projectile: something thrown or shot

vivid: producing strong mental images

Chapter 2

THINK THE GAME

Physical conditioning is important, but it is only one component of effective preparation. Mental preparation is equally, and perhaps more, important. Even if you are in peak physical condition, you will not succeed unless you have a firm grasp of the game plan and a confident, positive attitude.

Every coach has a set of plays and tactics they expect their players to know so well that they could run them in their sleep. Learning what plays to run at what times, as well as how to run them, makes players better teammates. They will be less likely to be out of position or make a costly mistake if they have mentally prepared and know what to do in any given situation.

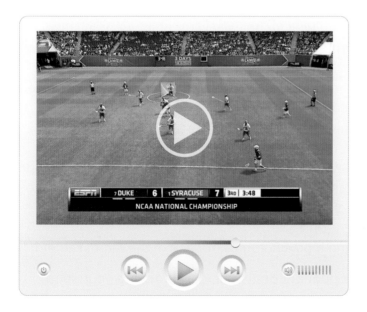

Offensive strategies and plays are broken down in this video.

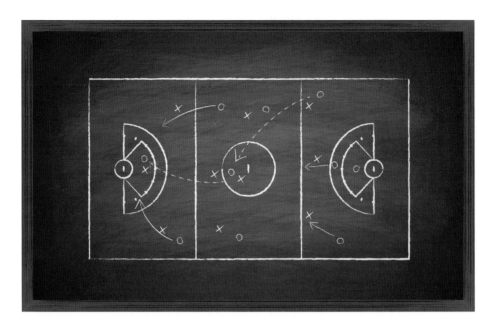

Even if players are in peak physical condition, that will be of limited use if they have not prepared and do not know the tactics of the game plan.

To develop confidence, many athletes use the technique of imagery. With your mind, you can create a **vivid** picture of what you want to happen: visualize yourself performing well technically without injury or mistake. For example, if you are concerned about an upcoming game in which you will be goalie, close your eyes, and picture yourself blocking shot after shot. Then, when it comes to the actual game, the fact that you have rehearsed your athletic performance in your mind's eye allows you to have the confidence you need to give it your all.

Sean Kelly, a Division I player at Fairfield University who now runs the Sports and Mental Preparation facility in New Jersey, offers the following advice for executing the technique of imagery.

- Construct in your mind a psychological replica of the lacrosse field.

- Place you and your opponent on that field, performing your sport.

- Build in the senses of sight, sound, and touch. The more senses involved in your mental imagery, the more successful it will be.

- You want to experience the faces of your opponents.

- You want to experience the energy in the arena.

- You want to experience yourself making the plays that will make the difference in the game.

Imagery is a key tool in developing a positive attitude. By visualizing what you want to achieve as a lacrosse player, your concentration and the determination to make your visions a reality can lead to an improved attitude. Sometimes pep talks by coaches or stories shared by other players can help you improve your optimism as well. No matter what, it is always important to stay focused: your teammates will be counting on you to give the game your full attention.

MENTAL APPROACH

Attitude is the mental approach, or mind-set, that athletes adopt toward their preparation. It often makes the difference in quality of play and even the outcome of a game. You should always try to maintain a positive attitude; there will be times that are more difficult than others, such as a rough practice or a losing game, but keeping a good outlook can help you keep things in perspective.

There are a lot of good reasons to play sports, including learning sportsmanship, the **camaraderie** of teammates, and developing discipline

and practice habits. Above all, however, sporting events are designed to be fun for players and spectators alike. Having fun should be the ultimate mind-set of players. Yes, you should take every game seriously, but winning or losing is less important than having fun and practicing good sportsmanship.

GEAR YOU NEED

Lacrosse has come a long way over the centuries, yet it is still basically, at its core, a stick and ball game. The original game of

Decades ago, a stick and a ball were all the equipment required to play lacrosse.

lacrosse played by Native Americans was rather simple: players only needed a ball and a lacrosse stick. However, as the sport has become more standardized and complex, so has its equipment.

As far as head protection goes, because men's lacrosse is full contact and therefore traditionally rougher than women's, helmets are required for all players. In women's lacrosse, only the goalie is required to wear a helmet, but it is an option for all players.

Women, however, do still get injured playing lacrosse. Just because helmets are not required and checking is not allowed does not mean that women's lacrosse is free of danger or that precautions do not need to be taken. According to an article published by the Center for Neuro Skills, "High rates of head and face injuries among women and increasing numbers of children learning to play lacrosse . . . is prompting another look at how much protective gear they need." A second study, conducted by the University of Virginia, discovered that "injuries to the head and face were significantly more prevalent among females (30.1 percent of all injuries) than among males (18 percent of all injuries), and often resulted from contact with the ball." Furthermore, "children ages four to eleven years old experienced the highest percent of injuries to the head and face of all lacrosse players." Clearly, lacrosse is a game in which safety must be considered a priority. The following safety equipment is either recommended or required. Check with your coach or league to be sure of specific requirements. Again, not all women's leagues require helmets, but using one is a smart idea.

Cleats, padded gloves, and elbow pads are all standard men's lacrosse equipment.

Data from the NCAA shows that concussions in women's lacrosse went down 11 percent between 2009 and 2013 from the levels in the prior five years. That is a notable improvement and certainly better than other women's sports like soccer, which had little change, and basketball, which saw an increase. At 5.5 concussions per 10,000 exposures, however, it is significantly worse than in the men's game, where the players wear helmets and suffered only 3.1 concussions per 10,000 exposures. Faced with the facts, the state of Florida mandated in 2015 that all high school girl players, not just the goalies as is traditional, had to wear protective headgear. This decision, however, was far from popular. Although girls play a no-bodychecking version of the game, critics argued that girls who felt safer when protected would play more aggressively on the field, therefore causing more injuries, the so-called gladiator effect. The statistics are hard to ignore, however. Only four high school sports, played by boys or girls, have higher concussion rates than girl's lacrosse. Part of the problem with the Florida rule is that the protection that was mandated is just a reinforced headband that protects only a small area of the head. Critics of the rule say it is not worth the hassle. Supporters of the rule say it did not go far enough. In 2016, U.S. Lacrosse adopted standards for an optional helmet with a half face shield. Time will tell if the sport with swinging sticks and an unforgiving projectile as its primary object ever decides that girls' heads need just as much protecting as boys'.

HEAD GEAR:

- Protective helmet, equipped with face mask, chin pad, and a cupped, four-point chin strap fastened to all four hookups (men)

- Proper eye protection, no helmets required (women)

- Helmet with a throat protector (all goalies)

- Mouthpiece that must be a highly visible color (all players)

BODY GEAR:

- Shoulder and arm pads required and rib pads strongly recommended (men, excluding goalies)

- Chest protector (all goalies)

- Padding on arms, legs, and shoulders that does not excessively increase the size of those body parts (recommended for all goalies) *High school level and below must wear padding on thighs and shins. *Youth level must wear some form of abdominal and pelvic protection (all goalies).

- padded gloves (all players)

- protective cup/jock strap (men)

- shoes with cleats (all players)

CHOOSING A STICK

Personal preference is the driving factor behind selecting a lacrosse stick for an individual player. The "right" lacrosse stick is, ultimately, the one that is best for your age, sex, position, and abilities. For men, lacrosse sticks usually have aluminum handles with either a traditional or mesh pocket (a traditional pocket is made of nylon and leather; a mesh pocket consists of woven nylon webbing). The depth of the pocket can vary, and the typical length of a men's lacrosse stick is thirty to sixty inches (seventy-six centimeters to one and a half meters) depending on the position played and personal preference. For women, lacrosse sticks have a traditional pocket, which is shallower than the pocket used by men. The pocket of a woman's lacrosse stick has stricter regulations, requiring four

> The trick to making your lacrosse stick an extension of yourself is just keeping it with you, keeping it by you, and growing that connection with it. Your stick is the most important tool for the game. It's what takes you to the next level. The better your skills are with your stick, the more comfortable you're going to be. Keep your stick in your hands. It will take you places.
>
> – Lyle Thompson, all-time NCAA men's career leader in points

or five leather or synthetic thongs (not both). Mesh is not allowed, and neither is more than two shooting strings. The typical length of a stick is thirty-six to forty-four inches (slightly shorter or longer than a meter).

CHOOSING A HELMET

Lacrosse is a full-contact sport, where players risk not only colliding with each other but also impacts from opponent sticks as well as the ball. Ideally, a lacrosse helmet should provide full protection to the face and neck. Also, lacrosse face guards must meet certain standards. For example, the wire mesh of the guard must protect the face but not be too close to it. This prevents the guard from smashing into the player's face in the case of a head-on collision. In addition, the chinstrap must be padded to protect the face.

A lacrosse helmet provides full protection for the head, face, and neck.

Along with protecting the head and face comes protecting the mouth. Mouth guards are usually attached directly to the helmet, but they can be sold separately as well. Mouth guards sold separately can be custom made for the player's mouth by a dentist. Mouth guards come preformed but eventually mold to the player's mouth with use over time. All types serve to protect the teeth and cushion blows to the head.

CHOOSING SHOES

Having good traction on the turf is an important element of the game, which is where a good pair of lacrosse shoes comes in. Lacrosse shoes are much the same for women and men. They are similar to a football or soccer shoe in that they have cleats. Cleats enable players to get better traction on the field, but they can also cause severe injuries if the players are not careful. Long cleats provide better grip but can lead to knee injuries: if the foot becomes firmly planted in the ground, it can be ripped away too quickly with a twisting motion or impact from another player, forcing the knee joint beyond its normal range of motion. Be sure to choose a cleat that will benefit you on the field but will not endanger your safety.

CHOOSING GLOVES

Lacrosse gloves are specifically designed to protect against the particular hazards of the sport. They have heavy padding on the tops of the fingers and around the wrist to protect the hands from being hit by a stick. The palm is made of leather, or a leather substitute, with thick pads around it for protection. Some players are known to cut the pads out of their gloves or purchase gloves without padding over the palms so that they can maintain a better grip on the stick. Do not do this without checking with your coach first.

Lacrosse gloves are padded to provide protection to the hands and wrists from being hit with opponents' sticks.

Use a tape measure to determine the distance from where your elbow pads will end to the tips of your fingers. This measurement equals your glove size, which will ensure that you get the gloves that fit you properly.

CHOOSING PADS

Due to the frequency of collision and the use of a hard **projectile** to play the game, lacrosse players wear a lot of upper body padding. The goalie, in particular, needs to make sure that the pads are snug and comfortable.

Pads are worn to protect the ribs and shoulders as well as the kidney area. To determine your correct shoulder and rib pad size, wrap a tape measure around your chest just below your armpits. This will indicate the size of pads you need.

Elbow pads serve to protect the arm from above the elbow to the forearm area where the top of the glove begins. Many are secured with adjustable Velcro® straps. To determine your correct elbow pad size, measure the distance between the edge of your shoulder pads and the cuff of your lacrosse glove. Note that the top of the elbow pad should leave no exposed skin between the shoulder pad and the glove.

EQUIPMENT CARE

Your equipment will last longer and do its job effectively if it is well maintained. Regularly check all your equipment, from your shoes to your stick, for wear and tear, and replace or repair immediately anything that is worn out, damaged, or ill fitting.

For safety, it is a good idea to check the playing or practice surface before using it. Check for holes or loose materials or debris. Anything unusual in the playing field should be brought to the attention of your coach or an

Lacrosse pads are designed to protect the shoulders, ribs, and kidneys. Elbow pads cover the area from halfway above the elbow to mid-forearm.

official because it could present a hazard, not just to you but also to all the players on the field.

Mental attitude and equipment are just two parts of the safety equation. Physical training is also vital, not only for skill and success on the lacrosse field but also for preparing your body for the demands of lacrosse.

TEXT-DEPENDENT QUESTIONS:

1. How is the equipment different for men and women in lacrosse?

2. A good lacrosse helmet should provide full protection to what two parts of the body?

3. How do you determine your correct elbow pad size?

RESEARCH PROJECT:

Put together a playbook diagraming your two favorite offensive or defensive plays or strategies, depending on your position. Then come up with a third play of your own design and include it in the book. Write an explanation outlining why you think the play will be effective.

 ## WORDS TO UNDERSTAND:

centrifugal: moving away from a center, acting in a direction away from a center

oblique: any of the thin flat muscles forming the middle and outer layers of the lateral walls of the abdomen

stamina: great physical or mental strength that allows you to continue doing something for a long time

Chapter 3

TRAIN FOR SUCCESS

Lacrosse is an extremely physical sport that puts intense demands on the body. During a typical college lacrosse game, each team takes seventy-five to eighty-five shots at the goals. For constant action like this, you need sharp reflexes and a body that can work quickly—and at the same time, you want to able to avoid injuries while playing.

ALWAYS WARM UP

Warming up is just as important as the rest of your drills or workouts. Without properly warming up each and every muscle before a game, you risk pulling a muscle or seriously injuring yourself in another way. Stretches are a good way to get your muscles ready to perform.

- Before stretching, run or jog lightly for a few minutes. This will help warm your muscles and allow for easier stretching; stretching a cold muscle is always more difficult.

- Each stretch should be held for a minimum of ten seconds. You can increase your flexibility by holding the stretches for longer periods of time—say twenty to thirty seconds.

- Do not bounce or jerk your muscles when you are stretching. While it may seem like you're helping to stretch out your muscles better, this can easily lead to tearing or spraining.

- Do not rush through stretching. This does your body no good and, again, can lead to injury. Always take the time to warm up properly.

- Listen to your body, and respect your limits. Gaining flexibility takes time; if something hurts excessively, stop right away. Don't be tempted to compare your stretching ability to anyone else's. Some bodies are naturally more flexible than others, and everyone has his or her own abilities and limits.

Here are some examples of stretches for different parts of the body.

UPPER BODY

- Stand with your legs shoulder width apart. Tuck your chin into your chest, and hold for fifteen seconds. Next, tilt your head toward your right shoulder and then your left, holding each for about fifteen seconds.

- Slowly rotate your head to the right and look over your shoulder until you feel a gentle stretch, hold for fifteen seconds, then repeat to the left.

- Stand with your feet shoulder width apart. Raise both arms above your head, and bend the left elbow and grasp it with the right hand. Pull your left upper arm gently toward the middle of your body. This should cause a stretch in your triceps. Hold for about fifteen seconds, and repeat with the opposite arm.

This triceps stretch is a good way to loosen the arm muscles before taking to the field for practice or games.

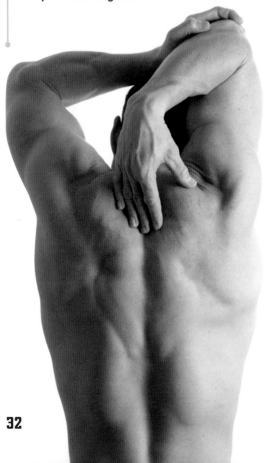

- Clasp your hands behind your back with your elbows fully extended. Lift your arms slightly, bend at the waist, then lift your arms up even further if you are able. Hold this stretch for ten seconds and repeat. This exercise stretches your shoulders and chest muscles.

LOWER BODY

- Sit on the floor with your legs stretched straight out in front of you, hip width apart. Keeping your legs as straight as you can, reach forward, and grab either your ankles or toes, depending on your level of flexibility. Hold for fifteen seconds. You should feel this stretch in the backs of your knees and lower back. Try it with your toes pointing straight up and pointing forward.

- Sit with your legs spread wide apart. Lean over your left leg, and grab your toes or left ankle. Point your toes forward, then back, and hold for another fifteen seconds. Switch sides and perform this stretch over your right leg.

- Stand with your feet shoulder width apart. Grab your right ankle, and pull it behind you toward your buttocks, bending your knee. You may need to hold onto a chair or wall for balance. Hold this stretch for fifteen seconds and repeat with the left leg.

- To perform what is known as the "butterfly stretch," sit on the floor with your knees bent and the soles of your feet pressed together. Hold your feet with your hands, then rest your elbows on your lower legs. Lean forward, and try to touch your nose to the floor, while you press down on your legs. Hold for fifteen to thirty seconds.

- Stand facing a wall, and place your hands at about shoulder height. Place one foot in front of the other, keeping the heel of your back foot planted firmly on the floor. Place your weight on your forward, bent leg, and then lean forward, as if you were trying to push against the wall. Hold for fifteen seconds, and repeat with the other leg.

The butterfly stretch is a good exercise to help increase flexibility in lacrosse players.

- For this second calf stretch, you will need a flight of stairs or a sturdy box. First, line up your heels with the edge of the step. Then, move your feet back so that the balls of your feet are on the edge of the step and the rest of your feet are hanging off the edge. Slowly dip your heels down and come back up. Repeat ten times.

- Stand with your legs shoulder width apart. Point your right toe so that it touches the ground, and roll your ankle in a clockwise direction three times. Then roll the ankle counterclockwise three times. Repeat with the left foot.

TRAINING AND CONDITIONING

Overall conditioning and training are important aspects for athletes in any sport. Athletes should also do training that is specific to the sport they play as well.

Lacrosse training can be further specialized by position. For example, defenders will be pushing attackers off their bodies, while attackers will be using pushing motions when facing off and also to secure elbow room and move around in a crush. Both will need strong triceps and strong pectorals, which are the thick muscles of the chest.

Strong shoulders and arms, along with good core strength, are also helpful in lacrosse. Muscles are strengthened effectively through weight and resistance training.

The incline press works the pectoral muscles to develop upper body strength.

Watch the Harvard men's lacrosse team hit the gym for a workout.

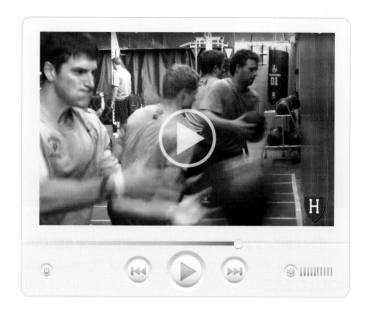

PECTORALS

Incline press with dumbbells: Lie on a weight bench that is at an angle; your shoulders should be higher than your buttocks. The weight bar should be supported on rests level with your chest. Grasp the weight bar with both hands, and lift the weight over your forehead and then back to your chest. Repeat as many times as possible, working up to a higher number each time.

ABDOMINALS

Core resistance exercise: Oblique crunches work the oblique muscles, which are on the sides of your abdominals. To perform them, lie on your back with your knees bent and your feet on the floor, with hands behind your head. Next, twist your legs to the right, and lower your knees to the floor. With your lower body in this position, raise your upper body, so your shoulders do not touch the floor, then slowly lower back down. Repeat ten to twenty times, then repeat the set. Then twist your legs to the left and repeat the crunching movement on the right side of the body.

- 30-60-90 box drill: Stand beside a twelve- to twenty-inch (thirty- to fifty-one-centimeter) box with feet shoulder width apart. Jump onto the box and back down to the ground on the opposite side, continuing back and forth across the box. Do thirty repetitions of one, two, or three, depending on your endurance level (making thirty, sixty, or ninety jumps total.)

CARDIO TRAINING

During both the off-season and your playing season, the training schedule that your coach sets up for you and your teammates will without a doubt include cardiovascular training, which improves stamina and endurance, vital components during a game. Something as simple as going for a thirty- to sixty-minute run on days that you don't have practice can improve your stamina.

SIDEBAR
The Lonely End of the Field

Goaltender is a solitary position. Their teammates abandon them regularly, leaving them alone in their goal crease to foray into enemy territory in search of the glory brought by goals. Goaltenders have accepted, and in most cases embraced, this existence, which often extends outside of games to practice. The offense does drills together, defenders work on their ground balls with each other, and the goalies? They are off by themselves or working with an assistant coach. It is lonely but important work. Here are three examples from goalie coach Damon Wilson of what goalies do to prepare.

EYE FOCUS DRILL
Position your head directly over your toes, looking down. With your top hand (the dominant hand), throw the ball very hard against the ground, and then catch it with the same hand. An alternative to this drill is to keep your eyes focused in the same spot (in between your feet) but bounce the ball outside of your feet, off to the side. This alternative will help develop peripheral vision.

AGILITY
Place two lacrosse sticks about four yards (three and a half meters) apart, parallel to one another. Start straddling one stick, and have your partner roll a

lacrosse ball from where you are to the other stick. Shuffle your feet to reach the other stick, then pick up the ball, and throw it back. Your partner then rolls the ball to the other side, and the drill repeats. Ensure you are going past the sticks every time. This drill works on conditioning, and about two sets of thirty reps should be good. Rest between sets, and then repeat.

WALL BALL WITH A SHORT STICK

Wall ball is a drill you can do when you're on your own. All you need is a stick, a ball, and a wall. Here is a short sample of the types of throws you can practice.

Standing about seven to ten feet (two to three meters) away from a concrete wall, perform thirty throws of each of the following. Try to limit yourself to a single cradle between each throw. You should attempt to throw the ball to the same spot on the wall every time so that the rebound comes up by your head.

- **Right Hand Overhand**

- **Left Hand Overhand**

- **Right Hand Overhead, Catch Left Side**—Throw across your body, so the rebound comes to the left side of your body. Keeping the right-handed grip on the stick, make the catch. and bring the stick back to the right side. Repeat

- **Left Hand Overhead, Catch Right Side**—Perform this the same way as the right-handed version except reversed.

- **Right Hand Side Arm**—Drop your release and catch point down to a sidearm.

- **Left Hand Side Arm**—Perform this the same as the right-handed version except reversed.

of this, squat down slightly, keeping the stick in front, and slide to the side of the stick. Step forward so you are in front of it, then slide to the other side of the stick, and step back behind it. This causes you to perform a sliding motion around the stick. Then, with the stick vertical in front of you, jump over it with both feet, and then jump back to the other side. Continue jumping back and forth for a few minutes, making sure that your knees are lifted high in the air when you jump. Finally, take several lacrosse sticks, cones, or whatever you can find that is handy, and place the objects in two lines, about one foot (thirteen centimeters) apart. Step forward between the objects with your knees as high as possible. This drill should feel and look a lot like the drill you see football players performing when they run along a row of tires, placing each foot in the middle of the tire.

- The next drill works on stick checking, the repeated tapping motion a defender uses to dislodge the ball from an opponent's stick. This drill, known as "Woody Woodpecker," helps teach the motion and control necessary for stick checking. You will need a partner for this exercise. One person should hold his or her stick horizontal to the ground, anywhere from hip to shoulder level, and the other person should hit the "opponent's" stick with his or her stick, using firm and rapid motions, like a woodpecker tapping on a tree. Try this in different positions, such as behind, forward, and to each side. When done, switch roles and repeat.

- The final defensive drill is a blocking drill known as "Monkey in the Middle." You will need two other people to practice this drill. They should stand facing each other about thirty feet (nine meters) apart. As the first person throws the ball to the second person, the person in the middle (the "monkey") should attempt to block the pass. If the monkey is successful in this attempt, the monkey takes possession. If unsuccessful, the monkey must quickly run around the first person and then head for the second person, trying to block the shot again. Basically, it is a game of keep-away. Be sure to take turns, alternating the position of "monkey."

Proper training combined with the right attitude and the right equipment goes a long way toward preventing injuries on the lacrosse field. No matter how carefully you prepare, however, sometimes injuries happen. When they do, it's important to know how to recover as quickly as possible, so you can get back on the field.

TEXT-DEPENDENT QUESTIONS:

1. Name a few examples of stretches aimed at the upper body. Now name some for the lower body.

2. Give one example of a plyometric exercise that is specific to lacrosse.

3. What is a simple way to improve your stamina on days that you don't have practice?

RESEARCH PROJECT:

Look into what is required to put together an effective off-season training program. What types of non-lacrosse activities are best to keep players in game shape? How might off-season training vary by position?

WORDS TO UNDERSTAND:

alleviate: to reduce the pain or trouble of (something), to make (something) less painful, difficult, or severe

debilitating: to make (someone or something) weak, to reduce the strength of (someone or something)

immobile: incapable of being moved

Chapter 4

TAKING CARE OF THE BODY: INJURIES AND NUTRITION

Stretching and warm-ups can help lacrosse players to prepare their bodies for the sudden movements and direction changes that are an integral part of the sport. In a collision sport like lacrosse, however, there are unavoidable impacts that can lead to acute injuries.

HAND AND WRIST INJURIES

Fractures, dislocations, and sprains are the most common injuries to the hand and wrist suffered by lacrosse players. These can occur as a result

A brace can be worn to support and stabilize a sprained wrist.

of a player falling to the ground, getting hit on the hand by another player's stick, or colliding with another player.

If you know or think you have experienced a break or fracture to a bone, seek immediate medical treatment. Until you can consult a physician, however, the usual treatment is to keep the injured area **immobile** and apply an ice pack for twenty to thirty minutes. Many finger fractures are not serious, especially those in the tip of the finger. Taping an injured finger to the healthy one next to it usually allows you to return to activity. If the fracture occurs in the second or third finger bone, however, a splint may be required, and it can take four to six weeks for the fracture to heal completely.

Finger dislocations, where the bones pop out of joint at the knuckles, are easy to diagnose. Common symptoms can include pain, a loss of mobility in the finger, and a noticeable deformity in the joint. Do not try to force the joint back into place yourself—you can potentially cause more damage. Instead, tape the dislocated finger to the healthy one next to it, and ice the area for periods of twenty to thirty minutes. Consult a physician to arrange for X-rays as soon as possible. These will determine the severity of the injury and establish whether there are fractures. Typically, you will have to wear a splint to immobilize the joint. Usually, recovery time is anywhere from six to twelve weeks.

Sprains are damage to the ligaments that connect the muscles in the hand and wrist. Typical symptoms include pain, swelling, and loss of mobility. This is not something that you should treat by yourself. For a finger, keep the joint immobile by taping it to a healthy finger, and apply ice for twenty-minute intervals until you can consult a physician. In most cases, treatment may consist of keeping the finger in a splint for two weeks. After that, it will be taped to a healthy finger until the injury is completely healed and full mobility is restored.

Ankle Sprains

Inversion **Normal** **Eversion**

Sprained Lateral Ligament

Sprained Medial Ligament

SHOULDERS

In lacrosse, many shoulder injuries are often overuse injuries and can occur as a result of the constant twisting and throwing motions that players engage in during the course of a game. Shoulder injuries are also common due to players being struck with a lacrosse stick or ball or landing heavily if they fall to the ground.

*Landing heavily after being knocked off balance
is a common cause of shoulder injuries in lacrosse.*

Lacrosse shoulder injuries run the gamut from less common fractures and dislocations to more frequent sprains and contusions. Fractures in the shoulder area almost always affect the collarbone, usually in the middle. A fractured collarbone is a serious injury. If you suspect such an injury, keep the arm still: immobilize it in a sling, and wrap a bandage around the arm so that it is kept close to the body. Ice may be applied for twenty-minute intervals until a doctor can be seen. Typical recovery time is anywhere from six to twelve weeks.

Joint stability is not what the shoulder is known for. In fact, the shoulder is the only joint in the body that is not held together by its ligaments. Rather, the few ligaments serve only to keep it from moving too far in any one direction. For that very reason, shoulder dislocations are common among lacrosse players. If the ball at the top of the upper arm bone comes out of the socket in the shoulder blade, symptoms include an obvious deformity of the shoulder, extreme pain, muscle spasms, and loss of mobility. You should not try to force the shoulder joint back in place or have anyone else try to do it for you. Instead, place your arm in a sling and ice the affected area for twenty-minute intervals until you can consult a doctor.

Of course, shoulder pads should always be worn, but the most effective way to help prevent the injuries discussed is to learn how to fall properly. Too often, when a person falls, the natural reaction is to hold out the arms to break the fall. This action, though, can lead to the very shoulder injuries just described. Instead, tuck in and roll with the fall rather than trying to break it. Your lacrosse coach or your doctor should be able to give you further instruction in this area.

THIGHS

Strains and bruises are the most common thigh injuries suffered by lacrosse players, particularly to the hamstring and quadriceps.

Hamstrings are the muscles at the back of the thigh between the knee and buttocks. They cause the knee to bend, therefore playing a vital role in walking, running, jumping, and controlling movement. A hamstring strain is one of the most common injuries, and one of the most **debilitating**, because it is such a large muscle group. Typical symptoms of a hamstring pull can include sharp pain and swelling and, in the most severe tears, bruising due to internal bleeding within the muscle. You may also be unable to raise your leg straight off the ground more than a short distance without feeling pain. Typical treatment includes rest, ice, and compression; usually resting for at least two or three days; icing the muscle for twenty minutes, three to four times a day; and wrapping the muscle in a compression bandage.

The quadriceps comprise the muscle group at the front of the thigh and can be strained, or more commonly, bruised due to impact. Injury symptoms include a sudden, stabbing pain in the front of the thigh, tenderness or possible discoloration on the front of the thigh, and pain when trying to straighten the knee. Typical treatment includes resting the injury for several days, icing to reduce swelling, wearing a compression bandage, then a gentle muscle stretching program to strengthen the muscles.

THE KNEE

Having strong quads and hamstrings is important as they serve to protect the knee, a complex joint with an intricate network of muscle, tendons, ligaments, cartilage, and bone, that assists in a variety of motions. Knee

Torn Anterior Cruciate Ligament (ACL)

Normal Knee

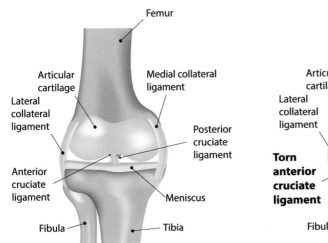

- Femur
- Articular cartilage
- Medial collateral ligament
- Lateral collateral ligament
- Posterior cruciate ligament
- Anterior cruciate ligament
- Meniscus
- Fibula
- Tibia

Knee with Torn ACL

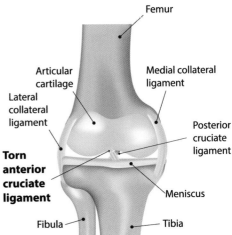

- Femur
- Articular cartilage
- Medial collateral ligament
- Lateral collateral ligament
- Posterior cruciate ligament
- **Torn anterior cruciate ligament**
- Meniscus
- Fibula
- Tibia

Torn knee ligaments are uncommon but serious lacrosse injuries that require immediate medical attention.

sprains are among the most common knee injuries seen in lacrosse players, and the recommended method of treatment is the familiar routine of resting, icing, and compressing the knee. Torn knee ligaments are another common and much more severe injury and require immediate medical attention.

CONCUSSIONS

Lacrosse is an impact sport where the potential for collision is high. Along with this comes the risk of the brain injury known as a concussion. Recent rule changes designed to prevent concussions in the men's game appear to have significantly reduced the incidence of these injuries. Data from the Datalys Center

Injuries from cuts and bruises to sprains and concussions can occur in a contact sport like lacrosse.

for Sports Injury Research and Prevention showed a 48 percent reduction in the average incidence of concussions in National Collegiate Athletic Association (NCAA) men's lacrosse from 2004–2009 to 2009–2013. Players with concussions should not play. Rest is the best treatment.

MINOR INJURIES

CUTS

- Grab the cleanest material you can find, such as a washcloth or a strip of gauze.

- Cover the cut with the cloth, and apply firm pressure to the wound. Maintain this pressure until the bleeding has stopped.

- Next, clean the wound gently with an antiseptic, and spread a thin layer of antibiotic ointment over the wound.

- If you cannot control the bleeding within a few minutes, seek medical help.

BRUISES

- Apply a cold compress or ice pack to the bruised area as soon as possible. Leave in place for fifteen minutes. Repeat at twenty-minute intervals over a period of at least four hours until swelling has stopped.

SPRAINS

- Apply a cold compress or ice pack as soon as possible. Leave in place for fifteen minutes. Repeat at twenty-minute intervals over a period of at least four hours until swelling has stopped.

- Elevate the sprained limb to at least waist level to help **alleviate** swelling.

- Once the swelling has stopped, soak the sprained area three times a day—first in warm water for twenty minutes then in icy water for twenty more minutes.

NUTRITION

Athletes depend on their bodies to perform on demand at a high level. Lacrosse is a high-energy, fast-paced game that requires strength and endurance. For players to perform optimally, the proper amount and type of fuel is required. Typically, an athlete has to eat considerably more than other people do to maintain higher energy levels. The United States Food and Drug Administration (FDA) suggests that the average American should eat about 2,000 calories a day; for a male high school- or college-level athlete, a 3,000- to 4,000-calorie diet is more common. There are three main food groups to consider when choosing a diet: carbohydrates, protein, and fats.

Virginia Tech's sports nutritionist shows the Hokies women's team how to make good food choices.

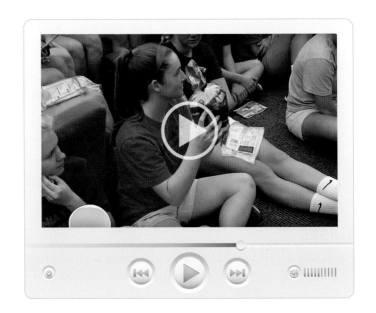

CARBOHYDRATES

Carbohydrates are foods rich in a chemical called starch, which is what the body breaks down to get energy. Starchy foods include breads and grains, vegetables such as potatoes, cereal, pasta, and rice. There is no one-size-fits-all formula that can exactly dictate what an athlete's carb consumption should be. A general rule is that in season or during times of intense training, athletes should eat about five grams of carbs for every pound of body weight. In the off-season or during periods of lower training levels, it should be about two to three grams per pound. The body uses carbs strictly for fuel, so if they are not being burned, they are turned into fat and stored. Therefore it is important to adjust carb intake based on activity level. Athletes should not eat heavily processed carbohydrates such as white

Carbohydrate intake should be adjusted to match activity levels. In season or during training, players should eat about five grams per pound of body weight daily, about double the off-season carb load.

sugar and white flour. These simple carbs are quickly broken down into sugars, which the body processes into fats if it does not immediately burn them off. The best carbohydrate choices for an athlete are complex types like pasta and whole grain foods as well as starchy vegetables. A nutritious diet avoids empty calories or those provided by food that lacks other nourishment, like processed sugar and starches.

> I always look to have at least two meals. If it's a night game, I have three meals. I like to bring fruit to the game to have after warm-ups, usually some berries, and a whole grain slice of bread with some almond butter.
>
> – Paul Rabil, three-time All-American midfielder

PROTEIN

Unlike carbohydrates, protein is used within the body. Proteins are important chemicals used to perform specific functions inside the body's cells. Our bodies can break down proteins that are found in foods and use them to build new proteins that make up our muscles and bones. During periods of intense training and activity, the body needs more protein to repair damage to muscles. Not eating enough protein can cause an athlete to lose muscle mass and negatively affect

the ability to perform. The Academy of Nutrition and Dietetics recommends athletes consume about one-half to three-quarters of a gram of protein for every pound of body weight. During the season or heavy training, that number should be closer to a full gram per pound. This higher ratio is also true if an athlete is trying to build muscle mass. The best sources of proteins are lean meats and dairy products (such as milk or cheese) as well as eggs and certain types of soy, beans, and nuts.

Lacrosse players need to eat a lot of protein to help build the muscle required to compete in the rough-and-tumble sport.

FATS

Lots of times, we think of fats as bad for us because eating too much of them is unhealthy. However, fat is an important ingredient needed to make our bodies work correctly. They help to balance hormone production, support cell growth, and protect your organs, among other functions. Without fats, our bodies cannot absorb certain vitamins as well as they should. Also, our skin and hair need some amount of fat to grow correctly. However, fat should still be eaten in moderation, as it is higher in calories than protein or carbs. No more than seventy grams a day is recommended. All fats are not created equal, however. Trans fats and saturated fats found in processed foods are high in bad cholesterol, which clogs arteries and is bad for the heart. The best sources of fat are vegetable oils, olive oil, and nuts.

Good fats like avocado, olive oil, and nuts are a necessary part of an athlete's diet.

Dietary supplements with vitamins and protein can help to fill the gaps and balance athletes' diets when they are having trouble finding time to eat right.

DIETARY SUPPLEMENTS

Ideally, a balanced diet would provide the body with all the nutrients it needs. However, for many varying factors, eating optimally is not always possible. Dietary supplements are available to fill dietary gaps created by a deficient diet.

In discussing dietary supplements here, this does not include banned performance-enhancing substances. Instead, the focus is on supplements that contain vitamins, minerals, and other compounds that help the body absorb nutrients or recover more efficiently. When properly used, supplements can improve overall health and performance, but you should always consult a doctor or other expert before using them to augment your diet or training program. Some examples of common supplements include vitamin tablets and protein shakes or powder.

VITAMINS

For many reasons, we do not always get the vitamins and nutrients we need. Often this is because our diets are not as balanced as they should be. Sometimes it is because the foods that are available to us have been processed in such a way that they lose nutrients. If you know or suspect that a certain key vitamin is underrepresented in what you are eating, in many cases, the necessary vitamins can be obtained from vitamin supplements. These supplements, which are usually taken as a pill, can either contain a balanced mixture of vitamins and nutrients (multivitamins) or contain a single vitamin or mineral that our diet is lacking. The best way to avoid this issue is to work hard to eat right whenever possible.

PROTEIN SUPPLEMENTS

Getting enough protein from the food you eat can be difficult as well. For athletes, eating protein immediately after a workout is recommended (to refuel your body), but most people either don't feel up to or do not have the time to spend cooking or preparing themselves a meal immediately after a workout. That is where protein shakes come in handy. These are protein supplements sold in powder form that look and taste like milkshakes when blended with water but contain no dairy products. Protein shakes deliver a high ratio of protein to carbohydrates and calories. They are not meant to replace meals. Many other necessary nutrients are gained from a balanced diet that cannot be replaced by protein shakes, regardless of how fortified they may be.

STAYING HYDRATED

The body needs water more than it needs any other nutrient. If you are not getting enough water, your performance will suffer in spite of any preparation or balanced diet. Dehydration occurs when your body doesn't have enough water. Symptoms include fatigue, dizziness, and headaches. No athlete can perform at his or her best if not properly hydrated. Proper hydration should be maintained not only at meets but throughout training as well. The body does not store water, so we need to constantly maintain its supply. The American College of Sports Medicine recommends these guidelines for athletes:

- **Before Exercise:** 16–20 ounces within the two-hour period prior to exercise

- **During Exercise:** 4–8 ounces every fifteen to twenty minutes during exercise

- **Post Exercise:** 24 ounces for every one pound of body weight lost during exercise

From attackers to goalies, no matter what the position or status on the team, if players want to perform well between the white lines, proper nutrition and hydration are important tools to help them succeed.

TEXT-DEPENDENT QUESTIONS:

1. Name the three most common injuries to the hand and wrist suffered by lacrosse players.

2. Having strong quads and hamstrings is important as they serve to protect what part of the body?

3. What nutrient helps balance hormone production, support cell growth, and protect your organs, among other functions?

RESEARCH PROJECT:

Put together a sample nutrition plan for yourself by mapping out meals and snacks for a given week. Pick a week when you are training and competing. Be sure to consider the nutrition benefits of everything you choose as well as the time it will take to make the plan work in your busy schedule.

WORDS TO UNDERSTAND:

accolades: awards or expressions of praise

lore: common or traditional knowledge or beliefs

lucrative: producing wealth

Chapter 5

LACROSSE: FROM NATIVE TRIBES TO NEW RULES AND THE NORTHEAST

ORIGINS AND EVOLUTION

Unlike relatively modern games like basketball and volleyball that have actual dates of invention, lacrosse is too old for anyone to know where it originated or when the first game was played.

Descriptions and depictions of stick and ball games go back for centuries, especially throughout the Americas. Native tribes in North America have particularly vivid legends with accounts of games that sound a lot like what we now know as lacrosse. One version comes from the **lore** of the Menominee people. According to their legend, a man called Manabozho arranged the first lacrosse match as a ruse to lure the gods of the underworld into the open, so he could exact revenge on them for the death of his brother.

These ancient legends were maintained through word of mouth, as were accounts of actual games as well. It was in eighteenth-century Quebec that French missionaries captured the first written accounts of both stories and observations of contests between tribes. In the next century, artist and author George Catlin captured his own observations of the sport on canvas. Catlin created hundreds of works during the 1830s capturing Native Americans engaged in the game those missionaries had described in their accounts.

Lacrosse was not just a game for the Native North American tribes that refined it. Primarily, it was a training exercise for young warriors in the tribe. The long, violent games tested and developed the strength and endurance of the tribe's young men. To mirror actual battle situations, it was common for the players not to eat during the games, which could go on for up to three days at a time. To prepare for games, players would eat only the meat

Before lacrosse games, Native American warriors followed a superstition of only eating the meat from fierce animals, like the grizzly bear.

of fierce animals, such as bears, rather than timid prey like rabbits or deer. As conflict grew between the two sides, the native tribes quickly learned how to take advantage of the fascination their European invaders had for the game. In June of 1763, unarmed Ojibwa warriors staged a game within sight of the walls of Fort Michilimackinac in Michigan. As the game raged on, the soldiers at the fort, most of them unarmed, wandered out to get a better look at the spectacle of the natives battling each other, leaving the gate open. Slowly, the play moved closer and closer to the fort. Before the soldiers realized what was happening, players became warriors, rushing the soldiers and overcoming them before they could get back through the gate, eventually capturing the fort.

The Ojibwa tribe captured Fort Michilimackinac in 1763 when they lured unsuspecting soldiers outside the gates by staging a lacrosse match nearby.

SIDEBAR
Lyle Thompson

There is a long list of firsts on Lyle Thompson's résumé. He was the first (and only) man to ever win back-to-back Enners Awards and back-to-back Tewaarton Awards, the first (and only) man to score 400 NCAA career points, and the first man to score 120 points in a NCAA season (he did it twice). The Florida Launch took Thompson first overall in the Major League Lacrosse (MLL) draft. And it was his first foray onto the social media site Twitter that got him his first taste of the national spotlight outside of lacrosse. Thompson is a Native American from the Onondaga Nation in upstate New York. His first post was to share a tweet by then presidential candidate Senator Bernie Sanders about an oil pipeline in North Dakota that the Sioux in that state were protesting. Since leaving college at Albany and turning pro, Thompson has been vocal about issues that affect Native Americans, such as the racist sports logos of the NFL team in Washington and the Major League Baseball (MLB) team in Cleveland. Thompson feels strongly about his heritage, having used the game of his ancestors to rise out of the depressed Onondaga Reservation to get a college education. His lacrosse exploits have made him a hero to his people. He just wants to give them a voice.

Aside from incorporating the game-in-war strategy, the tribes also used lacrosse to settle disputes. The best warriors from each tribe in disagreement would face each other in a game that was a complete free-for-all. The games had no rules and were therefore quite violent to the point where serious injury was common. Tackling, stick swinging, and full body contact were all part of the action.

The action itself took place in a carefully prepared playing area, usually an open field that was raked clear of loose stones and similar obstructions with a moose antler. The location was typically closer to the territory of one tribe or the other, so the visiting tribe would use the prepared field as a camping area before the competition. Games could have as many as a thousand players, with up to a hundred on the field at a time. Fields had no set boundaries, and the distance between goals could range from five hundred yards to several miles (one-half to several kilometers). Locations that were close to natural water sources like streams and rivers were preferred, so the players had an easy way to stay hydrated.

The tribes played with a variety of different sticks but all with a handle attached to a loop with either a carved-out wooden cup or webbing. Sticks were made of wood, with twisted bark or strips of animal skin for the webbing. Lacrosse balls were made of solid wood, clay, or stuffed animal hide.

Just as there was no standard equipment, there were also no standard rules. The only thing that was universal, whether watching Iroquois, Cherokee, or Seminoles play, is that no player could touch the ball with his hand. Over the centuries of European settlement, lacrosse evolved rules over time. In 1867 Montreal dentist Dr. William Beers, who grew up playing the game, proposed a formal set of regulations for the sport of lacrosse when he founded the Canadian National Lacrosse Foundation. They included the following:

- A team could field twelve players with no substitutions.

- The first team to lead by three goals or to reach five goals won.

- Goals were six feet by six feet (two meters by two meters) and recommended to be two hundred feet (sixty-one meters) apart.

- Balls could be no less than eight inches (twenty centimeters) but no more than ten inches (twenty-five centimeters) in circumference.

- Two on-field officials, called umpires, were stationed, one at each goal, while a referee followed the play up and down the field.

- Only the goalkeeper could touch the ball with a hand. Otherwise it was a foul. Other fouls included holding, tripping, making verbal threats, hitting opponents with a stick, or throwing a stick.

COLLEGE AND THE WOMEN'S GAME

Beers' organized version of the sport proved to be quite popular. By 1870, lacrosse clubs had sprung up around the Midwest and Northeast as well as in the southern and eastern parts of Ontario in the newly formed country of Canada. Beers was invited by the queen of England to put on a game at Windsor castle in 1876. That year, the *New York Herald* hailed the game as "the most remarkable, versatile, and exciting of all games of ball."

Perhaps the most significant event in modern lacrosse history took place in 1877, when teams representing Manhattan College and New York University (NYU) played a game against each other. This first college game, won by NYU, began the spread of the sport at the college level to Maryland and New Jersey. In 1882, the Intercollegiate Lacrosse Association was formed, with Ivy League schools Yale, Harvard, and Princeton as members. The sport failed to grow,

Queen Victoria of England invited Dr. William Beers to put on a lacrosse exhibition at Windsor castle in 1876.

The stick skills required in lacrosse are difficult to master, which some experts believe deter athletes and cause many to choose football or baseball instead.

however, and by the end of the century, all three schools had dropped lacrosse. The schools wanted to keep their best athletes in more popular and **lucrative** sports like football, crew, baseball, and track and field. Experts also speculate that the sport lost popularity with athletes. The stick skills required to be good at lacrosse are difficult to master compared to swinging a bat or throwing a spiral.

At smaller schools, however, lacrosse found its following and spread into these kinds of institutions. At Johns Hopkins University (JHU) in Baltimore, for example, lacrosse thrived. Many of the sport's modern innovations came out of JHU. Robert Abercrombie was a player for the Black and Blue (now the Blue Jays) at the turn of the century. He devised a short stick for attackmen that made it easier to make short passes. Abercrombie is also credited with putting a net on the goalposts.

At about the same time, women began to play the sport. The first organized women's club, appeared in Baltimore in 1926. The U.S. Women's Lacrosse Association was founded in 1931.

By 1933, the sport was ready to evolve again. In the men's game, the number of players on the field went from twelve to ten (this has never changed for the women's game), leaving the goalkeeper, three defenders, three midfielders, and three attackmen (two wingers and a center). The distance between goals was changed to two hundred forty feet (seventy-three meters), with sixty feet (eighteen meters) between the end boundary and the back of each goal.

The centers start the game with a battle for the ball at the center of the field called a face-off, similar to ice hockey. Players are permitted to carry

Boys wear helmets with full face shields and mouth guards to protect them in what can be a very rough sport.

the ball cradled in the net at the end of their sticks and can pass the ball to teammates or shoot it at the opposing goal with a throwing motion. Also like hockey, full-body contact, called bodychecking, is allowed, but there are rules. If the contact is deemed to be illegal by the referee, a foul may be called. Men play four 15-minute quarters; women play two 30-minute halves.

The equipment has evolved along with the rules. Sticks are now made from lightweight aluminum or titanium. Players use sticks anywhere from seventy-two inches (just under two meters) for defenders to forty inches (about one meter) for attackers. Helmets with a full facemask and mouth guard are mandatory for males, as are padded gloves. Females wear protective eyewear and a mouth guard.

After decades as a successful regional sport at the high school and collegiate levels, lacrosse turned pro in 2001. MLL is a professional league formed that year that fielded nine teams in 2016. The National Lacrosse League (NLL) has been a professional box lacrosse league since 1987. This is an indoor league that plays a miniaturized version of the outdoor game. The NLL had nine teams in 2016, which was also the inaugural season for women's professional lacrosse. The United Women's Lacrosse League debuted with four teams in Baltimore, Boston, Long Island, and Philadelphia.

> *Always have the butt end of the stick lower than the top. That allows the ball to sit really nicely in the top of your cage, and gives you a quicker release and a quicker chance to get the ball (on the draw).*
>
> – Taylor Cummings, two-time NCAA national champion and three-time Tewaarton Award winner

In lacrosse, stars are made and accolades are given at the collegiate level, for both men and women. The women's game now has more than a hundred sanctioned Division I NCAA programs. Of these, the programs at Northwestern University in Chicago and the University of Maryland have had the most success, winning at least seven titles since the first women's tournament in 1982.

Maryland's Jen Adams is one of the best players in the sport's history. Between 1998 and 2001, she racked up 445 points to become the all-time NCAA leader in career points for men or women. She led her team to the national title in all four of her years at Maryland. Other great Maryland players include three-time winner of the Teewarton Award for best player Taylor Cummings, defender Tracy Stumpf, and goalie Alex Kehoe.

Watch this tribute to Jen Adams from her Hall of Fame induction.

At Northwestern, the largest offensive legacy belongs to Hannah Nielsen. The attacker accrued 224 assists in her career from 2006 to 2009, an NCAA women's record. Like Adams, Nielsen also led her team to four straight national championships. Those Wildcats teams were so powerful that two of Nielsen's teammates, Shannon Smith and Kristen Kjellman, also scored more than three hundred career points.

Other notable female players in NCAA lacrosse history include Katie Rowan of Syracuse, Mary Key of Johns Hopkins, Gail Cummings of Temple, Rachel Becker of Princeton, Cherie Greer of Virginia, and Marsha Florio of Penn State.

INTO THE WEST AND THE FUTURE

On the men's side, the most successful Division I programs belong to Syracuse University, with ten national championships, and Baltimore's Johns Hopkins with nine. Both schools have a long and storied tradition of lacrosse excellence. Prior to the inception of the NCAA Men's Division I lacrosse tournament in 1971, the national champion was determined by a vote of the United States Intercollegiate Lacrosse Association from 1936 to 1972. Under this format, Johns Hopkins was awarded an additional eleven titles. All in all, JHU claims forty-four national titles from 1891 to 2016.

Lacrosse games start with a face-off between the two centers in the middle of the field.

The tradition of greatness at Johns Hopkins starts with Jack Turnbull, a three-time All-American who played as an attackman from 1929 to 1932. In that time, he was known as "the Babe Ruth of lacrosse." The current award for NCAA Attackman of the Year is named for Turnbull.

Del Dressel is one of only five four-time All-Americans in NCAA Division I lacrosse history. He played midfield at JHU, winning two McLaughlin awards as best midfielder in the country in 1984 and 1985.

As far as JHU defenders go, none was better than Dave Pietramala. He led the Blue Jays to the championship in 1987 and won an Enners award as the most outstanding player in the country in 1989. Pietramala went on to become the head coach at JHU, winning the title in 2005.

In goal, Larry Quinn made his mark on JHU lacrosse history by backstopping the team to back-to-back championships in 1984 and 1985. In 1984 the team was undefeated. Quinn won the Enners award in both seasons, the only goalie in history ever to win the award twice.

At Syracuse, which can claim four additional championships prior to 1971, the conversation starts with Jim Brown. The National Football League (NFL) superstar running back is also one of the best ever

Box lacrosse is played indoors in hockey arenas. The professional NLL, shown here, has been operating since 1987.

to play lacrosse. Brown played both football and lacrosse for Syracuse from 1954 to 1957. Syracuse lacrosse was unbeaten in Brown's senior year, when he was named an All-American.

One of Brown's teammates on that 1957 team was goaltender Oren Lyons, Jr. Lyons was one of the captains on that national championship team. He was inducted into the National Lacrosse Hall of Fame in 1992.

The other great Syracuse midfielder is Gary Gait. Gait is considered by many to be the best player ever at any position. No Division I midfielder has ever scored more goals. Gait won three NCAA titles, two McLaughlin awards, and an Enners award in his years at Syracuse from 1987 to 1990.

Up front, Syracuse had the firepower of the Powell brothers. Casey came first in 1995. He won a Turnbull award, two Enners awards, and a national championship in his years with the Orange. Mike Powell, Casey's younger brother, came to Syracuse in 2001 and was not only a four-year All-American but also history's only four-time Turnbull award winner as best attackman. He also won the Enners in 2004 and is Syracuse's all-time leading scorer. These two great programs, like most of the oldest and most successful men's programs, are located in America's Northeast. Every winner of the NCAA men's Division I lacrosse tournament has come from a school in the Eastern Time Zone, except for Denver in 2015. Despite this fact, the West may be where the future growth of the sport lies.

As the sport nears saturation levels in the Northeast, growth efforts will need to be focused to the West and South, and there is evidence this is happening. The National Federation of State High School

Oregon high school players compete in front of the goal. Between 2008 and 2013, participation in girl's high school lacrosse went up 19 percent.

Associations data shows that between 2008 and 2013, high school lacrosse participation grew 19 percent among girls and 15 percent among boys. Among sports with at least 10,000 participants, that is the fastest growth rate in the country. Between 2009 and 2013, the six largest growth regions were Florida, Georgia, Virginia, Minnesota, Ohio, and Michigan. In fact, the University of Michigan, a traditional football powerhouse, added men's lacrosse as a varsity program in 2012, the first Division I football school to do so since the University of Notre Dame way back in 1981.

This growth outside of the traditional lacrosse hotbeds of Maryland, Massachusetts, Delaware, Pennsylvania, New Hampshire, New York, New Jersey, and North Carolina will likely take some time. In Nebraska, for example, the state will not sanction lacrosse as an official sport until twenty high schools in neighboring states South Dakota, Iowa, Missouri, Kansas, Colorado, and Wyoming participate in the sport. This is a tall order in much of the South and Midwest, where football is the king of sports.

The great young players just keep coming, however. Loyola University's Pat Spencer established himself as a top-quality playmaker as an attackman for the Baltimore college in 2016, leading the Greyhounds to the Final Four. Up at Syracuse, standout freshman Nicole Levy scored forty-six goals and sixty-eight points and helped the Orange make the 2016 women's Final Four, earning All-Tournament honors as an attacker.

Spencer and Levy are just examples of the depth of talented players that continue to pursue the sport in increasing numbers, giving lacrosse a promising future.

TEXT-DEPENDENT QUESTIONS:

1. According to the Menominee people, who arranged the first lacrosse match as a ruse to lure the gods of the underworld into the open, so he could exact revenge on them for the death of his brother?

2. Which woman has the largest offensive legacy at Northwestern?

3. Which two universities have a long and storied tradition of men's lacrosse excellence?

RESEARCH PROJECT:

Look up the biggest stars of the early years of college lacrosse, from 1936 to 1970. Choose one player, and write a profile of him, briefly outlining his early years from discovering the game through high school and detailing his accomplishments at the collegiate level, indicating his impact on the sport. Why was this player significant in lacrosse history?

SERIES GLOSSARY OF KEY TERMS

Acute Injury: Usually the result of a specific impact or traumatic event that occurs in one specific area of the body, such as a muscle, bone, or joint.

Calories: units of heat used to indicate the amount of energy that foods will produce in the human body.

Carbohydrates: substances found in certain foods (such as bread, rice, and potatoes) that provide the body with heat and energy and are made of carbon, hydrogen, and oxygen.

Cardiovascular: of or relating to the heart and blood vessels.

Concussion: a stunning, damaging, or shattering effect from a hard blow—especially a jarring injury of the brain resulting in a disturbance of cerebral function.

Confidence: faith in oneself and one's abilities without any suggestion of conceit or arrogance.

Cooldown: easy exercise, done after more intense activity, to allow the body to gradually transition to a resting or near-resting state.

Dietary Supplements: products taken orally that contain one or more ingredient (such as vitamins or amino acids) that are intended to supplement one's diet and are not considered food.

Dynamic: having active strength of body or mind.

Electrolytes: substances (such as sodium or calcium) that are ions in the body regulating the flow of nutrients into and waste products out of cells.

Flexible: applies to something that can be readily bent, twisted, or folded without any sign of injury.

Hamstrings: any of three muscles at the back of the thigh that function to flex and rotate the leg and extend the thigh.

Hydration: to supply with ample fluid or moisture.

Imagery: mental images, the products of imagination.

Mind-Set: a mental attitude or inclination.

Overuse Injury: an injury that is most likely to occur to the ankles, knees, hands, and wrists, due to the excessive use of these body parts during exercise and athletics.

Plyometrics: also known as "jump training" or "plyos," exercises in which muscles exert maximum force in short intervals of time, with the goal of increasing power (speed and strength).

Positive Mental Attitude (PMA): the philosophy that having an optimistic disposition in every situation in one's life attracts positive changes and increases achievement.

Protein: a nutrient found in food (as in meat, milk, eggs, and beans) that is made up of many amino acids joined together, is a necessary part of the diet, and is essential for normal cell structure and function.

Quadriceps: the greater extensor muscle of the front of the thigh that is divided into four parts.

Recovery: the act or process of becoming healthy after an illness or injury.

Resistance: relating to exercise, involving pushing against a source of resistance (such as a weight) to increase strength. Strength training, or resistance exercises, are those that build muscle. They create stronger and larger muscles by producing more and tougher muscle fibers to cope with the increasing weight demands.

Strategy: a careful plan or method.

Stretching: to extend one's body or limbs from a cramped, stooping, or relaxed position.

Tactics: actions or methods that are planned and used to achieve a particular goal.

Tendon: a tough piece of tissue in the body that connects a muscle to a bone.

Training: the process by which an athlete prepares for competition by exercising, practicing, and so on.

Warm-Up: exercise or practice especially before a game or contest—broadly, to get ready.

Workout: a practice or exercise to test or improve one's fitness for athletic competition, ability, or performance.

FURTHER READING:

Brandon, Leigh. *Anatomy of Sports Injuries: For Fitness and Rehabilitation.* London, UK: New Holland Publishers, 2013.

Fisher, Donald M. *Lacrosse: A History of the Game.* Baltimore, MD: Johns Hopkins University Press, 2011.

Luke, Andrew. *Lacrosse (Inside the World of Sports).* Broomall, PA: Mason Crest, 2017.

Zimmerman, Don. *Men's Lacrosse.* Champaign, IL: Human Kinetics, 2013.

INTERNET RESOURCES:

Stop Sports Injuries: *http://www.stopsportsinjuries.org/STOP/Prevent_Injuries/Lacrosse_Injury_Prevention.aspx*

Inside Lacrosse: *http://www.insidelacrosse.com/*

FDA: Dietary Supplements: *http://www.fda.gov/Food/DietarySupplements/default.htm*

VIDEO CREDITS:

Check out this pro tip on how to play one-on-one defense: *http://x-qr.net/1H80*

Offensive strategies and plays are broken down in this video: *http://x-qr.net/1HGb*

Watch the Harvard men's lacrosse team hit the gym for a workout: *http://x-qr.net/1HKE*

Virginia Tech's sports nutritionist shows the Hokies women's team how to make good food choices: *http://x-qr.net/1FoT*

Watch this tribute to Jen Adams from her Hall of Fame induction: *http://x-qr.net/1DSE*

PICTURE CREDITS

QR CODES AND LINKS TO THIRD-PARTY CONTENT

INDEX

In this index, page numbers in **bold italics** font indicate photos or videos.

ABOUT THE AUTHOR

Peter Douglas is a former journalist, reporting on both sports and general news for many years at television stations in various locations across the US affiliated with NBC, CBS and Fox. Prior to his journalism career he worked with the Boston Red Sox Major League baseball team. An avid writer and sports enthusiast, he has authored 16 additional books on sports topics. In his downtime Peter enjoys family time with his wife and two young children and attending hockey and baseball games in his home city.